Merry Christmas, Christine!
  Love,
Edward and Margaret Cox

2006

psalms

psalms

VIKING
an imprint of
PENGUIN BOOKS

VIKING

Published by the Penguin Group
Penguin Group (Australia)
250 Camberwell Road, Camberwell, Victoria 3124, Australia
(a division of Pearson Australia Group Pty Ltd)
Penguin Group (USA) Inc.
375 Hudson Street, New York, New York 10014, USA
Penguin Group (Canada)
90 Eglinton Avenue East, Suite 700, Toronto ON M4P 2Y3, Canada
(a division of Pearson Penguin Canada Inc.)
Penguin Books Ltd
80 Strand, London WC2R 0RL, England
Penguin Ireland
25 St Stephen's Green, Dublin 2, Ireland
(a division of Penguin Books Ltd)
Penguin Books India Pvt Ltd
11 Community Centre, Panchsheel Park, New Delhi – 110 017, India
Penguin Group (NZ)
Cnr Airborne and Rosedale Roads, Albany, Auckland, New Zealand
(a division of Pearson New Zealand Ltd)
Penguin Books (South Africa) (Pty) Ltd
24 Sturdee Avenue, Rosebank, Johannesburg 2196, South Africa

Penguin Books Ltd, Registered Offices: 80 Strand, London, WC2R 0RL, England

First published by Penguin Group (Australia), a division of Pearson Australia Group
Pty Ltd, 2005

10 9 8 7 6 5 4 3 2 1

Text selection copyright © Penguin Group (Australia) 2005

The moral right of the author has been asserted

All rights reserved. Without limiting the rights under copyright reserved above,
no part of this publication may be reproduced, stored in or introduced into
a retrieval system, or transmitted, in any form or by any means (electronic,
mechanical, photocopying, recording or otherwise), without the prior written
permission of both the copyright owner and the above publisher of this book.

Cover design by Adam Laszczuk © Penguin Group (Australia)
Text design by Claire Tice © Penguin Group (Australia)

Cover photograph by Getty Images
Typeset in Aldus by Post Pre-press Group, Queensland
Printed in China by Everbest Printing Co. Ltd

National Library of Australia
Cataloguing-in-Publication data:

Bible. O.T. Psalms. English.
Psalms.

Gift ed.
ISBN 0 670 02855 X

I. Title.

223.2

www.penguin.com.au

Contents

Introduction	1
Psalms of Prayer & Worship	3
Psalms of Lament	39
Psalms of Thanksgiving	89
Index of First Lines	119

Introduction

Central to the Christian and Jewish faiths, the Book of Psalms is the prayer book of the Bible. Historically, the psalms played a significant role in the ritual life of the people of ancient Israel, and were originally created to be ongoing elements of worship within religious communities – prayers set to music. The psalms still play a central role in modern religious ceremonies, and are recited and sung at all occasions.

The Book of Psalms consists of 150 chapters, inspired by the heights and depths of human experience. Chapters were written by different people at different times between 500 and 100 BC, but most are attributed to David. This collection brings together 100 of the most popular and moving psalms, exploring themes of praise and worship, lament, and thanksgiving.

The psalms of praise and worship are hymns to praise God and a celebration of faith. They declare universal truths about the experience of faith, and are imbued with the joyful belief that God's actions are evident and touch humanity deeply.

The majority of the psalms are songs of lament – pleas for God's help in times of trouble. They acknowledge and express the intensity of human suffering, and provide a means with which to communicate deep feelings of grief and despair, while still expressing a trust in God.

Psalms of thanksgiving express joyous appreciation for God's work. They are distinguished from the psalms of praise and worship by being a direct response to a particular action – an acknowledgement that a prayer has been answered.

The psalms are beautiful, poetic modes of expression, and communicate deep, resonant human emotions. They speak to all aspects of the human condition and are as timely today as when they were first written. This rich treasury gives reason to reflect upon our humanity through times of joy, sorrow, contemplation and celebration.

Psalms of Prayer & Worship

1

1. Blessed is the man that walketh not in the counsel of the ungodly, nor standeth in the way of sinners, nor sitteth in the seat of the scornful.
2. But his delight is in the law of the Lord; and in his law doth he meditate day and night.
3. And he shall be like a tree planted by the rivers of water, that bringeth forth his fruit in his season; his leaf also shall not wither; and whatsoever he doeth shall prosper.
4. The ungodly are not so: but are like the chaff which the wind driveth away.
5. Therefore the ungodly shall not stand in the judgment, nor sinners in the congregation of the righteous.
6. For the Lord knoweth the way of the righteous: but the way of the ungodly shall perish.

2

1 Why do the heathen rage, and the people imagine a vain thing?
2 The kings of the earth set themselves, and the rulers take counsel together, against the Lord, and against his anointed, saying,
3 Let us break their bands asunder, and cast away their cords from us.
4 He that sitteth in the heavens shall laugh: the Lord shall have them in derision.
5 Then shall he speak unto them in his wrath, and vex them in his sore displeasure.
6 Yet have I set my king upon my holy hill of Zion.
7 I will declare the decree: the Lord hath said unto me, Thou art my Son; this day have I begotten thee.
8 Ask of me, and I shall give thee the heathen for thine inheritance, and the uttermost parts of the earth for thy possession.
9 Thou shalt break them with a rod of iron; thou shalt dash them in pieces like a potter's vessel.
10 Be wise now therefore, O ye kings: be instructed, ye judges of the earth.
11 Serve the Lord with fear, and rejoice with trembling.
12 Kiss the Son, lest he be angry, and ye perish from the way, when his wrath is kindled but a little. Blessed are all they that put their trust in him.

24

1. The earth is the Lord's, and the fulness thereof; the world, and they that dwell therein.
2. For he hath founded it upon the seas, and established it upon the floods.
3. Who shall ascend into the hill of the Lord? Or who shall stand in his holy place?
4. He that hath clean hands, and a pure heart; who hath not lifted up his soul unto vanity, nor sworn deceitfully.
5. He shall receive the blessing from the Lord, and righteousness from the God of salvation.
6. This is the generation of them that seek him, that seek thy face, O Jacob.
7. Lift up your heads, O ye gates; and be ye lift up, ye everlasting doors; and the King of glory shall come in.
8. Who is this King of glory? The Lord strong and mighty, the Lord mighty in battle.
9. Lift up your heads, O ye gates; even lift them up, ye everlasting doors; and the King of glory shall come in.
10. Who is this King of glory? The Lord of hosts, he is the King of glory.

29

1. Give unto the Lord, O ye mighty, give unto the Lord glory and strength.
2. Give unto the Lord the glory due unto his name; worship the Lord in the beauty of holiness.
3. The voice of the Lord is upon the waters: the God of glory thundereth: the Lord is upon many waters.
4. The voice of the Lord is powerful; the voice of the Lord is full of majesty.
5. The voice of the Lord breaketh the cedars; yea, the Lord breaketh the cedars of Lebanon.
6. He maketh them also to skip like a calf; Lebanon and Sirion like a young unicorn.
7. The voice of the Lord divideth the flames of fire.
8. The voice of the Lord shaketh the wilderness; the Lord shaketh the wilderness of Kadesh.
9. The voice of the Lord maketh the hinds to calve, and discovereth the forests: and in his temple doth every one speak of his glory.
10. The Lord sitteth upon the flood; yea, the Lord sitteth King for ever.
11. The Lord will give strength unto his people; the Lord will bless his people with peace.

45

1. My heart is inditing a good matter: I speak of the things which I have made touching the king: my tongue is the pen of a ready writer.
2. Thou art fairer than the children of men: grace is poured into thy lips: therefore God hath blessed thee for ever.
3. Gird thy sword upon thy thigh, O most mighty, with thy glory and thy majesty.
4. And in thy majesty ride prosperously because of truth and meekness and righteousness; and thy right hand shall teach thee terrible things.
5. Thine arrows are sharp in the heart of the king's enemies; whereby the people fall under thee.
6. Thy throne, O God, is for ever and ever: the sceptre of thy kingdom is a right sceptre.
7. Thou lovest righteousness, and hatest wickedness: therefore God, thy God, hath anointed thee with the oil of gladness above thy fellows.
8. All thy garments smell of myrrh, and aloes, and cassia, out of the ivory palaces, whereby they have made thee glad.
9. Kings' daughters were among thy honourable women: upon thy right hand did stand the queen in gold of Ophir.

10 Hearken, O daughter, and consider, and incline thine ear; forget also thine own people, and thy father's house;
11 So shall the king greatly desire thy beauty: for he is thy Lord; and worship thou him.
12 And the daughter of Tyre shall be there with a gift; even the rich among the people shall intreat thy favour.
13 The king's daughter is all glorious within: her clothing is of wrought gold.
14 She shall be brought unto the king in raiment of needlework: the virgins her companions that follow her shall be brought unto thee.
15 With gladness and rejoicing shall they be brought: they shall enter into the king's palace.
16 Instead of thy fathers shall be thy children, whom thou mayest make princes in all the earth.
17 I will make thy name to be remembered in all generations: therefore shall the people praise thee for ever and ever.

46

1. God is our refuge and strength, a very present help in trouble.
2. Therefore will not we fear, though the earth be removed, and though the mountains be carried into the midst of the sea;
3. Though the waters thereof roar and be troubled, though the mountains shake with the swelling thereof.
4. There is a river, the streams whereof shall make glad the city of God, the holy place of the tabernacles of the most High.
5. God is in the midst of her; she shall not be moved: God shall help her, and that right early.
6. The heathen raged, the kingdoms were moved: he uttered his voice, the earth melted.
7. The Lord of hosts is with us; the God of Jacob is our refuge.
8. Come, behold the works of the Lord, what desolations he hath made in the earth.
9. He maketh wars to cease unto the end of the earth; he breaketh the bow, and cutteth the spear in sunder; he burneth the chariot in the fire.
10. Be still, and know that I am God: I will be exalted among the heathen, I will be exalted in the earth.
11. The Lord of hosts is with us; the God of Jacob is our refuge.

47

1. O clap your hands, all ye people; shout unto God with the voice of triumph.
2. For the Lord most high is terrible; he is a great King over all the earth.
3. He shall subdue the people under us, and the nations under our feet.
4. He shall choose our inheritance for us, the excellency of Jacob whom he loved.
5. God is gone up with a shout, the Lord with the sound of a trumpet.
6. Sing praises to God, sing praises: sing praises unto our King, sing praises.
7. For God is the King of all the earth: sing ye praises with understanding.
8. God reigneth over the heathen: God sitteth upon the throne of his holiness.
9. The princes of the people are gathered together, even the people of the God of Abraham: for the shields of the earth belong unto God: he is greatly exalted.

48

1. Great is the Lord, and greatly to be praised in the city of our God, in the mountain of his holiness.
2. Beautiful for situation, the joy of the whole earth, is mount Zion, on the sides of the north, the city of the great King.
3. God is known in her palaces for a refuge.
4. For, lo, the kings were assembled, they passed by together.
5. They saw it, and so they marvelled; they were troubled, and hasted away.
6. Fear took hold upon them there, and pain, as of a woman in travail.
7. Thou breakest the ships of Tarshish with an east wind.
8. As we have heard, so have we seen in the city of the Lord of hosts, in the city of our God: God will establish it for ever.
9. We have thought of thy loving kindness, O God, in the midst of thy temple.
10. According to thy name, O God, so is thy praise unto the ends of the earth: thy right hand is full of righteousness.
11. Let mount Zion rejoice, let the daughters of Judah be glad, because of thy judgments.
12. Walk about Zion, and go round about her: tell the towers thereof.

13 Mark ye well her bulwarks, consider her palaces; that ye may tell it to the generation following.
14 For this God is our God for ever and ever: he will be our guide even unto death.

49

1. Hear this, all ye people; give ear, all ye inhabitants of the world:
2. Both low and high, rich and poor, together.
3. My mouth shall speak of wisdom; and the meditation of my heart shall be of understanding.
4. I will incline mine ear to a parable: I will open my dark saying upon the harp.
5. Wherefore should I fear in the days of evil, when the iniquity of my heels shall compass me about?
6. They that trust in their wealth, and boast themselves in the multitude of their riches;
7. None of them can by any means redeem his brother, nor give to God a ransom for him:
8. (For the redemption of their soul is precious, and it ceaseth for ever:)
9. That he should still live for ever, and not see corruption.
10. For he seeth that wise men die, likewise the fool and the brutish person perish, and leave their wealth to others.
11. Their inward thought is, that their houses shall continue for ever, and their dwelling places to all generations; they call their lands after their own names.
12. Nevertheless man being in honour abideth not: he is like the beasts that perish.
13. This their way is their folly: yet their posterity approve their sayings.

14 Like sheep they are laid in the grave; death shall feed on them; and the upright shall have dominion over them in the morning; and their beauty shall consume in the grave from their dwelling.
15 But God will redeem my soul from the power of the grave: for he shall receive me.
16 Be not thou afraid when one is made rich, when the glory of his house is increased;
17 For when he dieth he shall carry nothing away: his glory shall not descend after him.
18 Though while he lived he blessed his soul: and men will praise thee, when thou doest well to thyself.
19 He shall go to the generation of his fathers; they shall never see light.
20 Man that is in honour, and understandeth not, is like the beasts that perish.

50

1. The mighty God, even the Lord, hath spoken, and called the earth from the rising of the sun unto the going down thereof.
2. Out of Zion, the perfection of beauty, God hath shined.
3. Our God shall come, and shall not keep silence: a fire shall devour before him, and it shall be very tempestuous round about him.
4. He shall call to the heavens from above, and to the earth, that he may judge his people.
5. Gather my saints together unto me; those that have made a covenant with me by sacrifice.
6. And the heavens shall declare his righteousness: for God is judge himself.
7. Hear, O my people, and I will speak; O Israel, and I will testify against thee: I am God, even thy God.
8. I will not reprove thee for thy sacrifices or thy burnt offerings, to have been continually before me.
9. I will take no bullock out of thy house, nor he goats out of thy folds.
10. For every beast of the forest is mine, and the cattle upon a thousand hills.
11. I know all the fowls of the mountains: and the wild beasts of the field are mine.
12. If I were hungry, I would not tell thee: for the world is mine, and the fulness thereof.

13 Will I eat the flesh of bulls, or drink the blood of goats?
14 Offer unto God thanksgiving; and pay thy vows unto the most High:
15 And call upon me in the day of trouble: I will deliver thee, and thou shalt glorify me.
16 But unto the wicked God saith, What hast thou to do to declare my statutes, or that thou shouldest take my covenant in thy mouth?
17 Seeing thou hatest instruction, and casteth my words behind thee.
18 When thou sawest a thief, then thou consentedst with him, and hast been partaker with adulterers.
19 Thou givest thy mouth to evil, and thy tongue frameth deceit.
20 Thou sittest and speakest against thy brother; thou slanderest thine own mother's son.
21 These things hast thou done, and I kept silence; thou thoughtest that I was altogether such an one as thyself: but I will reprove thee, and set them in order before thine eyes.
22 Now consider this, ye that forget God, lest I tear you in pieces, and there be none to deliver.
23 Whoso offereth praise glorifieth me: and to him that ordereth his conversation aright will I shew the salvation of God.

73

1. Truly God is good to Israel, even to such as are of a clean heart.
2. But as for me, my feet were almost gone; my steps had well nigh slipped.
3. For I was envious at the foolish, when I saw the prosperity of the wicked.
4. For there are no bands in their death: but their strength is firm.
5. They are not in trouble as other men; neither are they plagued like other men.
6. Therefore pride compasseth them about as a chain; violence covereth them as a garment.
7. Their eyes stand out with fatness: they have more than heart could wish.
8. They are corrupt, and speak wickedly concerning oppression: they speak loftily.
9. They set their mouth against the heavens, and their tongue walketh through the earth.
10. Therefore his people return hither: and waters of a full cup are wrung out to them.
11. And they say, How doth God know? and is there knowledge in the most High?
12. Behold, these are the ungodly, who prosper in the world; they increase in riches.

13 Verily I have cleansed my heart in vain, and washed my hands in innocency.
14 For all the day long have I been plagued, and chastened every morning.
15 If I say, I will speak thus; behold, I should offend against the generation of thy children.
16 When I thought to know this, it was too painful for me;
17 Until I went into the sanctuary of God; then understood I their end.
18 Surely thou didst set them in slippery places: thou castedst them down into destruction.
19 How are they brought into desolation, as in a moment! they are utterly consumed with terrors.
20 As a dream when one awaketh; so, O Lord, when thou awakest, thou shalt despise their image.
21 Thus my heart was grieved, and I was pricked in my reins.
22 So foolish was I, and ignorant: I was as a beast before thee.
23 Nevertheless I am continually with thee: thou hast holden me by my right hand.
24 Thou shalt guide me with thy counsel, and afterward receive me to glory.
25 Whom have I in heaven but thee? and there is none upon earth that I desire beside thee.
26 My flesh and my heart faileth: but God is the strength of my heart, and my portion for ever.

27 For, lo, they that are far from thee shall perish: thou hast destroyed all them that go a whoring from thee.
28 But it is good for me to draw near to God: I have put my trust in the Lord God, that I may declare all thy works.

81

1 Sing aloud unto God our strength: make a joyful noise unto the God of Jacob.
2 Take a psalm, and bring hither the timbrel, the pleasant harp with psaltery.
3 Blow up the trumpet in the new moon, in the time appointed, on our solemn feast day.
4 For this was a statute for Israel, and a law of the God of Jacob.
5 This he ordained in Joseph for a testimony, when he went out through the land of Egypt: where I heard a language that I understood not.
6 I removed his shoulder from the burden: his hands were delivered from the pots.
7 Thou calledst in trouble, and I delivered thee; I answered thee in the secret place of thunder: I proved thee at the waters of Meribah.
8 Hear, O my people, and I will testify unto thee: O Israel, if thou wilt hearken unto me;
9 There shall no strange god be in thee; neither shalt thou worship any strange god.
10 I am the Lord thy God, which brought thee out of the land of Egypt: open thy mouth wide, and I will fill it.
11 But my people would not hearken to my voice; and Israel would none of me.

12 So I gave them up unto their own hearts' lust: and they walked in their own counsels.
13 Oh that my people had hearkened unto me, and Israel had walked in my ways!
14 I should soon have subdued their enemies, and turned my hand against their adversaries.
15 The haters of the Lord should have submitted themselves unto him: but their time should have endured for ever.
16 He should have fed them also with the finest of the wheat: and with honey out of the rock should I have satisfied thee.

82

1. God standeth in the congregation of the mighty; he judgeth among the gods.
2. How long will ye judge unjustly, and accept the persons of the wicked?
3. Defend the poor and fatherless: do justice to the afflicted and needy.
4. Deliver the poor and needy: rid them out of the hand of the wicked.
5. They know not, neither will they understand; they walk on in darkness: all the foundations of the earth are out of course.
6. I have said, Ye are gods; and all of you are children of the most High.
7. But ye shall die like men, and fall like one of the princes.
8. Arise, O God, judge the earth: for thou shalt inherit all nations.

84

1. How amiable are thy tabernacles, O Lord of hosts!
2. My soul longeth, yea, even fainteth for the courts of the Lord: my heart and my flesh crieth out for the living God.
3. Yea, the sparrow hath found a house, and the swallow a nest for herself, where she may lay her young, even thine altars, O Lord of hosts, my King, and my God.
4. Blessed are they that dwell in thy house: they will be still praising thee.
5. Blessed is the man whose strength is in thee; in whose heart are the ways of them.
6. Who passing through the valley of Baca make it a well; the rain also filleth the pools.
7. They go from strength to strength, every one of them in Zion appeareth before God.
8. O Lord God of hosts, hear my prayer; give ear, O God of Jacob.
9. Behold, O God our shield, and look upon the face of thine anointed.
10. For a day in thy courts is better than a thousand. I had rather be a doorkeeper in the house of my God, than to dwell in the tents of wickedness.
11. For the Lord God is a sun and shield: the Lord will give grace and glory: no good thing will he withhold from them that walk uprightly.

12 O Lord of hosts, blessed is the man that trusteth in thee.

93

1. The Lord reigneth, he is clothed with majesty; the Lord is clothed with strength, wherewith he hath girded himself: the world also is established, that it cannot be moved.
2. Thy throne is established of old: thou art from everlasting.
3. The floods have lifted up, O Lord, the floods have lifted up their voice; the floods lift up their waves.
4. The Lord on high is mightier than the noise of many waters, yea, than the mighty waves of the sea.
5. Thy testimonies are very sure: holiness becometh thine house, O Lord, for ever.

96

1. O sing unto the Lord a new song: sing unto the Lord, all the earth.
2. Sing unto the Lord, bless his name; shew forth his salvation from day to day.
3. Declare his glory among the heathen, his wonders among all people.
4. For the Lord is great, and greatly to be praised: he is to be feared above all gods.
5. For all the gods of the nations are idols: but the Lord made the heavens.
6. Honour and majesty are before him: strength and beauty are in his sanctuary.
7. Give unto the Lord, O ye kindreds of the people, give unto the Lord glory and strength.
8. Give unto the Lord the glory due unto his name: bring an offering, and come into his courts.
9. O worship the Lord in the beauty of holiness: fear before him, all the earth.
10. Say among the heathen that the Lord reigneth: the world also shall be established that it shall not be moved: he shall judge the people righteously.
11. Let the heavens rejoice, and let the earth be glad; let the sea roar, and the fulness thereof.
12. Let the field be joyful, and all that is therein: then shall all the trees of the wood rejoice.

13 Before the Lord: for he cometh, for he cometh to judge the earth: he shall judge the world with righteousness, and the people with his truth.

97

1. The Lord reigneth; let the earth rejoice; let the multitude of isles be glad thereof.
2. Clouds and darkness are round about him: righteousness and judgment are the habitation of his throne.
3. A fire goeth before him, and burneth up his enemies round about.
4. His lightnings enlightened the world: the earth saw, and trembled.
5. The hills melted like wax at the presence of the Lord, at the presence of the Lord of the whole earth.
6. The heavens declare his righteousness, and all the people see his glory.
7. Confounded be all they that serve graven images, that boast themselves of idols: worship him, all ye gods.
8. Zion heard, and was glad; and the daughters of Judah rejoiced because of thy judgments, O Lord.
9. For thou, Lord, art high above all the earth: thou art exalted far above all gods.
10. Ye that love the Lord, hate evil: he preserveth the souls of his saints; he delivereth them out of the hand of the wicked.
11. Light is sown for the righteous, and gladness for the upright in heart.
12. Rejoice in the Lord, ye righteous; and give thanks at the remembrance of his holiness.

98

1. O sing unto the Lord a new song; for he hath done marvellous things: his right hand, and his holy arm, hath gotten him the victory.
2. The Lord hath made known his salvation: his righteousness hath he openly shewed in the sight of the heathen.
3. He hath remembered his mercy and his truth toward the house of Israel: all the ends of the earth have seen the salvation of our God.
4. Make a joyful noise unto the Lord, all the earth: make a loud noise, and rejoice, and sing praise.
5. Sing unto the Lord with the harp; with the harp, and the voice of a psalm.
6. With trumpets and sound of cornets make a joyful noise before the Lord, the King.
7. Let the sea roar, and the fulness thereof; the world, and they that dwell therein.
8. Let the floods clap their hands: let the hills be joyful together.
9. Before the Lord; for he cometh to judge the earth: with righteousness shall he judge the world, and the people with equity.

101

1. I will sing of mercy and judgment: unto thee, O Lord, will I sing.
2. I will behave myself wisely in a perfect way. O when wilt thou come unto me? I will walk within my house with a perfect heart.
3. I will set no wicked thing before mine eyes: I hate the work of them that turn aside; it shall not cleave to me.
4. A froward heart shall depart from me: I will not know a wicked person.
5. Whoso privily slandereth his neighbour, him will I cut off: him that hath a high look and a proud heart will not I suffer.
6. Mine eyes shall be upon the faithful of the land, that they may dwell with me: he that walketh in a perfect way, he shall serve me.
7. He that worketh deceit shall not dwell within my house: he that telleth lies shall not tarry in my sight.
8. I will early destroy all the wicked of the land; that I may cut off all wicked doers from the city of the Lord.

112

1. Praise ye the Lord. Blessed is the man that feareth the Lord, that delighteth greatly in his commandments.
2. His seed shall be mighty upon earth: the generation of the upright shall be blessed.
3. Wealth and riches shall be in his house: and his righteousness endureth for ever.
4. Unto the upright there ariseth light in the darkness: he is gracious, and full of compassion, and righteous.
5. A good man sheweth favour, and lendeth: he will guide his affairs with discretion.
6. Surely he shall not be moved for ever: the righteous shall be in everlasting remembrance.
7. He shall not be afraid of evil tidings: his heart is fixed, trusting in the Lord.
8. His heart is established, he shall not be afraid, until he see his desire upon his enemies.
9. He hath dispersed, he hath given to the poor; his righteousness endureth for ever; his horn shall be exalted with honour.
10. The wicked shall see it, and be grieved; he shall gnash with his teeth, and melt away: the desire of the wicked shall perish.

122

1 I was glad when they said unto me, Let us go into the house of the Lord.
2 Our feet shall stand within thy gates, O Jerusalem.
3 Jerusalem is builded as a city that is compact together:
4 Whither the tribes go up, the tribes of the Lord, unto the testimony of Israel, to give thanks unto the name of the Lord.
5 For there are set thrones of judgment, the thrones of the house of David.
6 Pray for the peace of Jerusalem: they shall prosper that love thee.
7 Peace be within thy walls, and prosperity within thy palaces.
8 For my brethren and companions' sakes, I will now say, Peace be within thee.
9 Because of the house of the Lord our God I will seek thy good.

127

1. Except the Lord build the house, they labour in vain that build it: except the Lord keep the city, the watchman waketh but in vain.
2. It is vain for you to rise up early, to sit up late, to eat the bread of sorrows: for so he giveth his beloved sleep.
3. Lo, children are an heritage of the Lord: and the fruit of the womb is his reward.
4. As arrows are in the hand of a mighty man, so are children of the youth.
5. Happy is the man that hath his quiver full of them: they shall not be ashamed, but they shall speak with the enemies in the gate.

128

1 Blessed is every one that feareth the Lord; that walketh in his ways.
2 For thou shalt eat the labour of thine hands: happy shalt thou be, and it shall be well with thee.
3 Thy wife shall be as a fruitful vine by the sides of thine house: thy children like olive plants round about thy table.
4 Behold, that thus shall the man be blessed that feareth the Lord.
5 The Lord shall bless thee out of Zion: and thou shalt see the good of Jerusalem all the days of thy life.
6 Yea, thou shalt see thy children's children, and peace upon Israel.

133

1 Behold, how good and how pleasant it is for brethren to dwell together in unity!
2 It is like the precious ointment upon the head, that ran down upon the beard, even Aaron's beard: that went down to the skirts of his garments;
3 As the dew of Hermon, and as the dew that descended upon the mountains of Zion: for there the Lord commanded the blessing, even life for evermore.

134

1 Behold, bless ye the Lord, all ye servants of the Lord, which by night stand in the house of the Lord.
2 Lift up your hands in the sanctuary, and bless the Lord.
3 The Lord that made heaven and earth bless thee out of Zion.

Psalms of Lament

3

1 Lord, how are they increased that trouble me! many are they that rise up against me.
2 Many there be which say of my soul, There is no help for him in God.
3 But thou, O Lord, art a shield for me; my glory, and the lifter up of mine head.
4 I cried unto the Lord with my voice, and he heard me out of his holy hill.
5 I laid me down and slept; I awaked; for the Lord sustained me.
6 I will not be afraid of ten thousands of people, that have set themselves against me round about.
7 Arise, O Lord; save me, O my God: for thou hast smitten all mine enemies upon the cheek bone; thou hast broken the teeth of the ungodly.
8 Salvation belongeth unto the Lord: thy blessing is upon thy people.

4

1. Hear me when I call, O God of my righteousness: thou hast enlarged me when I was in distress; have mercy upon me, and hear my prayer.
2. O ye sons of men, how long will ye turn my glory into shame? how long will ye love vanity, and seek after leasing?
3. But know that the Lord hath set apart him that is godly for himself: the Lord will hear when I call unto him.
4. Stand in awe, and sin not: commune with your own heart upon your bed, and be still.
5. Offer the sacrifices of righteousness, and put your trust in the Lord.
6. There be many that say, Who will shew us any good? Lord, lift thou up the light of thy countenance upon us.
7. Thou hast put gladness in my heart, more than in the time that their corn and their wine increased.
8. I will both lay me down in peace, and sleep: for thou, Lord, only makest me dwell in safety.

6

1. O Lord rebuke me not in thine anger, neither chasten me in thy hot displeasure.
2. Have mercy upon me, O Lord; for I am weak: O Lord, heal me; for my bones are vexed.
3. My soul is also sore vexed: but thou, O Lord, how long?
4. Return, O Lord, deliver my soul: oh save me for thy mercies' sake.
5. For in death there is no remembrance of thee: in the grave who shall give thee thanks?
6. I am weary with my groaning; all the night make I my bed to swim; I water my couch with my tears.
7. Mine eye is consumed because of grief; I waxeth old because of all mine enemies.
8. Depart from me, all ye workers of iniquity; for the Lord hath heard the voice of my weeping.
9. The Lord hath heard my supplication; the Lord will receive my prayer.
10. Let all mine enemies be ashamed and sore vexed: let them return and be ashamed suddenly.

7

1 O Lord my God, in thee do I put my trust: save me from all them that persecute me, and deliver me:
2 Lest he tear my soul like a lion, rending it in pieces, while there is none to deliver.
3 O Lord my God, If I have done this; if there be iniquity in my hands;
4 If I have rewarded evil unto him that was at peace with me; (yea, I have delivered him that without cause is mine enemy:)
5 Let the enemy persecute my soul, and take it; yea, let him tread down my life upon the earth, and lay mine honour in the dust.
6 Arise, O Lord, in thine anger, lift up thyself because of the rage of mine enemies: and awake for me to the judgment that thou hast commanded.
7 So shall the congregation of the people compass thee about: for their sakes therefore return thou on high.
8 The Lord shall judge the people: judge me, O Lord, according to my righteousness, and according to mine integrity that is in me.
9 Oh let the wickedness of the wicked come to an end; but establish the just: for the righteous God trieth the hearts and reins.
10 My defence is of God, which saveth the upright in heart.

11 God judgeth the righteous, and God is angry with the wicked every day.
12 If he turn not, he will whet his sword; he hath bent his bow, and made it ready.
13 He hath also prepared for him the instruments of death; he ordaineth his arrows against the persecutors.
14 Behold, he travaileth with iniquity, and hath conceived mischief, and brought forth falsehood.
15 He made a pit, and digged it, and is fallen into the ditch which he made.
16 His mischief shall return upon his own head, and his violent dealing shall come down upon his own pate.
17 I will praise the Lord according to his righteousness: and will sing praise to the name of the Lord most high.

9

1. I will praise thee, O Lord, with my whole heart; I will shew forth all thy marvellous works.
2. I will be glad and rejoice in thee: I will sing praise to thy name, O thou most High.
3. When mine enemies are turned back, they shall fall and perish at thy presence.
4. For thou hast maintained my right and my cause; thou satest in the throne judging right.
5. Thou hast rebuked the heathen, thou hast destroyed the wicked, thou hast put out their name for ever and ever.
6. O thou enemy, destructions are come to a perpetual end: and thou hast destroyed cities; their memorial is perished with them.
7. But the Lord shall endure for ever: he hath prepared his throne for judgment.
8. And he shall judge the world in righteousness, he shall minister judgment to the people in uprightness.
9. The Lord also will be a refuge for the oppressed, a refuge in times of trouble.
10. And they that know thy name will put their trust in thee: for thou, Lord, hast not forsaken them that seek thee.
11. Sing praises to the Lord, which dwelleth in Zion: declare among the people his doings.

12 When he maketh inquisition for blood, he remembereth them: he forgetteth not the cry of the humble.
13 Have mercy upon me, O Lord; consider my trouble which I suffer of them that hate me, thou that liftest me up from the gates of death:
14 That I may shew forth all thy praise in the gates of the daughter of Zion: I will rejoice in thy salvation.
15 The heathen are sunk down in the pit that they made: in the net which they hid is their own foot taken.
16 The Lord is known by the judgment which he executeth: the wicked is snared in the work of his own hands. Higgaion.
17 The wicked shall be turned into hell, and all the nations that forget God.
18 For the needy shall not always be forgotten: the expectation of the poor shall not perish for ever.
19 Arise, O Lord; let not man prevail: let the heathen be judged in thy sight.
20 Put them in fear, O Lord: that the nations may know themselves to be but men.

10

1. Why standest thou afar off, O lord? why hidest thou thyself in times of trouble?
2. The wicked in his pride doth persecute the poor: let them be taken in the devices that they have imagined.
3. For the wicked boasteth of his heart's desire, and blesseth the covetous, whom the Lord abhorreth.
4. The wicked, through the pride of his countenance, will not seek after god: God is not in all his thoughts.
5. His ways are always grievous; thy judgments are far above out of his sight: as for all his enemies, he puffeth at them.
6. He hath said in his heart, I shall not be moved: for I shall never be in adversity.
7. His mouth is full of cursing and deceit and fraud: under his tongue is mischief and vanity.
8. He sitteth in the lurking places of the villages: in the secret places doth he murder the innocent: his eyes are privily set against the poor.
9. He lieth in wait secretly as a lion in his den: he lieth in wait to catch the poor: he doth catch the poor, when he draweth him into his net.
10. He croucheth, and humbleth himself, that the poor may fall by his strong ones.
11. He hath said in his heart, God hath forgotten: he hideth his face; he will never see it.

12 Arise, O Lord; O God, lift up thine hand: forget not the humble.
13 Wherefore doth the wicked contemn God? he hath said in his heart, Thou wilt not require it.
14 Thou hast seen it; for thou beholdest mischief and spite, to requite it with thy hand: the poor committeth himself unto thee; thou art the helper of the fatherless.
15 Break thou the arm of the wicked and the evil man: seek out his wickedness till thou find none.
16 The Lord is King for ever and ever: the heathen are perished out of his land.
17 Lord, thou hast heard the desire of the humble: thou wilt prepare their heart, thou wilt cause thine ear to hear:
18 To judge the fatherless and the oppressed, that the man of the earth may no more oppress.

13

1. How long wilt thou forget me, O Lord? for ever? how long wilt thou hide thy face from me?
2. How long shall I take counsel in my soul, having sorrow in my heart daily? how long shall mine enemy be exalted over me?
3. Consider and hear me, O Lord my God: lighten mine eyes, lest I sleep the sleep of death;
4. Lest mine enemy say, I have prevailed against him; and those that trouble me rejoice when I am moved.
5. But I have trusted in thy mercy; my heart shall rejoice in thy salvation.
6. I will sing unto the Lord, because he hath dealt bountifully with me.

17

1. Hear the right, O Lord, attend unto my cry, give ear unto my prayer, that goeth not out of feigned lips.
2. Let my sentence come forth from thy presence; let thine eyes behold the things that are equal.
3. Thou hast proved mine heart; thou hast visited me in the night; thou hast tried me, and shalt find nothing; I am purposed that my mouth shall not transgress.
4. Concerning the works of men, by the word of thy lips I have kept me from the paths of the destroyer.
5. Hold up my goings in thy paths, that my footsteps slip not.
6. I have called upon thee, for thou wilt hear me, O God: incline thine ear unto me, and hear my speech.
7. Shew thy marvellous loving kindness, O thou that savest by thy right hand them which put their trust in thee from those that rise up against them.
8. Keep me as the apple of the eye, hide me under the shadow of thy wings.
9. From the wicked that oppress me, from my deadly enemies, who compass me about.
10. They are inclosed in their own fat: with their mouth they speak proudly.
11. They have now compassed us in our steps: they have set their eyes bowing down to the earth;

12 Like as a lion that is greedy of his prey, and as it were a young lion lurking in secret places.
13 Arise, O Lord, disappoint him, cast him down: deliver my soul from the wicked, which is thy sword:
14 From men which are thy hand, O Lord, from men of the world, which have their portion in this life, and whose belly thou fillest with thy hid treasure: they are full of children, and leave the rest of their substance to their babes.
15 As for me, I will behold thy face in righteousness: I shall be satisfied, when I awake, with thy likeness.

22

1. My God, my God, why hast thou forsaken me? why art thou so far from helping me, and from the words of my roaring?
2. O my God, I cry in the daytime, but thou hearest not; and in the night season, and am not silent.
3. But thou art holy, O thou that inhabitest the praises of Israel.
4. Our fathers trusted in thee: they trusted, and thou didst deliver them.
5. They cried unto thee, and were delivered: they trusted in thee, and were not confounded.
6. But I am a worm, and no man; a reproach of men, and despised of the people.
7. All they that see me laugh me to scorn: they shoot out the lip, they shake the head, saying,
8. He trusted on the Lord that he would deliver him; let him deliver him, seeing he delighted in him.
9. But thou art he that took me out of the womb: thou didst make me hope when I was upon my mother's breasts.
10. I was cast upon thee from the womb: thou art my God from my mother's belly.
11. Be not far from me; for trouble is near; for there is none to help.

12 Many bulls have compassed me: strong bulls of Bashan have beset me round.
13 They gaped upon me with their mouths, as a ravening and a roaring lion.
14 I am poured out like water, and all my bones are out of joint: my heart is like wax; it is melted in the midst of my bowels.
15 My strength is dried up like a potsherd; and my tongue cleaveth to my jaws; and thou hast brought me into the dust of death.
16 For dogs have compassed me: the assembly of the wicked have inclosed me: they pierced my hands and my feet.
17 I may tell all my bones: they look and stare upon me.
18 They part my garments among them, and cast lots upon my vesture.
19 But be not thou far from me, O Lord: O my strength, haste thee to help me.
20 Deliver my soul from the sword; my darling from the power of the dog.
21 Save me from the lion's mouth: for thou hast heard me from the horns of the unicorns.
22 I will declare thy name unto my brethren: in the midst of the congregation will I praise thee.
23 Ye that fear the Lord, praise him; all ye the seed of Jacob, glorify him; and fear him, all ye the seed of Israel.

24 For he hath not despised nor abhorred the affliction of the afflicted; neither hath he hid his face from him; but when he cried unto him, he heard.
25 My praise shall be of thee in the great congregation: I will pay my vows before them that fear him.
26 The meek shall eat and be satisfied: they shall praise the Lord that seek him: your heart shall live for ever.
27 All the ends of the world shall remember and turn unto the Lord: and all the kindreds of the nations shall worship before thee.
28 For the kingdom is the Lord's: and he is the governor among the nations.
29 All they that be fat upon earth shall eat and worship: all they that go down to the dust shall bow before him: and none can keep alive his own soul.
30 A seed shall serve him; it shall be accounted to the Lord for a generation.
31 They shall come, and shall declare his righteousness unto a people that shall be born, that he hath done this.

25

1. Unto thee, O Lord, do I lift up my soul.
2. O my God, I trust in thee: let me not be ashamed, let not mine enemies triumph over me.
3. Yea, let none that wait on thee be ashamed: let them be ashamed which transgress without cause.
4. Shew me thy ways, O Lord; teach me thy paths.
5. Lead me in thy truth, and teach me: for thou art the God of my salvation; on thee do I wait all the day.
6. Remember, O Lord, thy tender mercies and thy lovingkindnesses; for they have been ever of old.
7. Remember not the sins of my youth, nor my transgressions: according to thy mercy remember thou me for thy goodness' sake, O Lord.
8. Good and upright is the Lord: therefore will he teach sinners in the way.
9. The meek will he guide in judgment: and the meek will he teach his way.
10. All the paths of the Lord are mercy and truth unto such as keep his covenant and his testimonies.
11. For thy name's sake, O Lord, pardon mine iniquity; for it is great.
12. What man is he that feareth the Lord? him shall he teach in the way that he shall choose.
13. His soul shall dwell at ease; and his seed shall inherit the earth.

14 The secret of the Lord is with them that fear him; and he will shew them his covenant.
15 Mine eyes are ever toward the Lord; for he shall pluck my feet out of the net.
16 Turn thee unto me, and have mercy upon me; for I am desolate and afflicted.
17 The troubles of my heart are enlarged: O bring thou me out of my distresses.
18 Look upon mine affliction and my pain; and forgive all my sins.
19 Consider mine enemies; for they are many; and they hate me with cruel hatred.
20 O keep my soul, and deliver me: let me not be ashamed; for I put my trust in thee.
21 Let integrity and uprightness preserve me; for I wait on thee.
22 Redeem Israel, O God, out of all his troubles.

26

1 Judge me, O Lord; for I have walked in mine integrity: I have trusted also in the Lord; therefore I shall not slide.
2 Examine me, O Lord, and prove me; try my reins and my heart.
3 For thy loving kindness is before mine eyes: and I have walked in thy truth.
4 I have not sat with vain persons, neither will I go in with dissemblers.
5 I have hated the congregation of evildoers; and will not sit with the wicked.
6 I will wash mine hands in innocency: so will I compass thine altar, O Lord:
7 That I may publish with the voice of thanksgiving, and tell of all thy wondrous works.
8 Lord, I have loved the habitation of thy house, and the place where thine honour dwelleth.
9 Gather not my soul with sinners, nor my life with bloody men:
10 In whose hands is mischief, and their right hand is full of bribes.
11 But as for me, I will walk in mine integrity: redeem me, and be merciful unto me.
12 My foot standeth in an even place: in the congregations will I bless the Lord.

27

1. The Lord is my light and my salvation; whom shall I fear? the Lord is the strength of my life; of whom shall I be afraid?
2. When the wicked, even mine enemies and my foes, came upon me to eat up my flesh, they stumbled and fell.
3. Though a host should encamp against me, my heart shall not fear: though war should rise against me, in this will I be confident.
4. One thing have I desired of the Lord, that will I seek after; that I may dwell in the house of the Lord all the days of my life, to behold the beauty of the Lord, and to enquire in his temple.
5. For in the time of trouble he shall hide me in his pavilion: in the secret of his tabernacle shall he hide me; he shall set me up upon a rock.
6. And now shall mine head be lifted up above mine enemies round about me: therefore will I offer in his tabernacle sacrifices of joy; I will sing, yea, I will sing praises unto the Lord.
7. Hear, O Lord, when I cry with my voice: have mercy also upon me, and answer me.
8. When thou saidst, Seek ye my face; my heart said unto thee, Thy face, Lord, will I seek.

9 Hide not thy face far from me; put not thy servant away in anger: thou hast been my help; leave me not, neither forsake me, O God of my salvation.
10 When my father and mother forsake me, then the Lord will take me up.
11 Teach me thy way, O Lord, and lead me in a plain path, because of mine enemies.
12 Deliver me not over unto the will of mine enemies: for false witnesses are risen up against me, and such as breathe out cruelty.
13 I had fainted, unless I had believed to see the goodness of the Lord in the land of the living.
14 Wait on the Lord: be of good courage, and he shall strengthen thine heart: wait, I say, on the Lord.

31

1 In thee, O Lord, do I put my trust; let me never be ashamed: deliver me in thy righteousness.
2 Bow down thine ear to me; deliver me speedily: be thou my strong rock, for an house of defence to save me.
3 For thou art my rock and fortress; therefore for thy name's sake lead me, and guide me.
4 Pull me out of the net that they have laid privily for me: for thou art my strength.
5 Into thine hand I commit my spirit: thou hast redeemed me, O Lord God of truth.
6 I have hated them that regard lying vanities: but I trust in the Lord.
7 I will be glad and rejoice in thy mercy: for thou hast considered my trouble; thou hast known my soul in adversities;
8 And hast not shut me up into the hand of the enemy: thou hast set my feet in a large room.
9 Have mercy upon me, O Lord, for I am in trouble; mine eye is consumed with grief, yea, my soul and my belly.
10 For my life is spent with grief, and my years with sighing: my strength faileth because of mine iniquity, and my bones are consumed.

11 I was a reproach among all mine enemies, but especially among my neighbours, and a fear to mine acquaintance: they that did see me without fled from me.
12 I am forgotten as a dead man out of mind: I am like a broken vessel.
13 For I have heard the slander of many: fear was on every side: while they took counsel together against me, they devised to take away my life.
14 But I trusted in thee, O Lord: I said, Thou art my God.
15 My times are in thy hand: deliver me from the hand of mine enemies, and from them that persecute me.
16 Make thy face to shine upon thy servant: save me for thy mercies' sake.
17 Let me not be ashamed, O Lord; for I have called upon thee: let the wicked be ashamed, and let them be silent in the grave.
18 Let the lying lips be put to silence; which speak grievous things proudly and contemptuously against the righteous.
19 Oh how great is thy goodness, which thou hast laid up for them that fear thee; which thou hast wrought for them that trust in thee before the sons of men!
20 Thou shalt hide them in the secret of thy presence from the pride of man: thou shalt keep them secretly in a pavilion from the strife of tongues.
21 Blessed be the Lord: for he hath shewed me his marvellous kindness in a strong city.

22 For I said in my haste, I am cut off from before thine eyes: nevertheless thou heardest the voice of my supplications when I cried unto thee.
23 O love the Lord, all ye his saints: for the Lord preserveth the faithful, and plentifully rewardeth the proud doer.
24 Be of good courage, and he shall strengthen your heart, all ye that hope in the Lord.

51

1. Have mercy upon me, O God, according to thy loving kindness: according unto the multitude of thy tender mercies blot out my transgressions.
2. Wash me thoroughly from mine iniquity, and cleanse me from my sin.
3. For I acknowledge my transgressions: and my sin is ever before me.
4. Against thee, thee only, have I sinned, and done this evil in thy sight: that thou mightest be justified when thou speakest, and be clear when thou judgest.
5. Behold, I was shapen in iniquity; and in sin did my mother conceive me.
6. Behold, thou desirest truth in the inward parts: and in the hidden part thou shalt make me to know wisdom.
7. Purge me with hyssop, and I shall be clean: wash me, and I shall be whiter than snow.
8. Make me to hear joy and gladness; that the bones which thou hast broken may rejoice.
9. Hide thy face from my sins, and blot out all mine iniquities.
10. Create in me a clean heart, O God; and renew a right spirit within me.
11. Cast me not away from thy presence; and take not thy holy spirit from me.

12 Restore unto me the joy of thy salvation: and uphold me with thy free spirit.

13 Then will I teach transgressors thy ways; and sinners shall be converted unto thee.

14 Deliver me from bloodguiltiness, O God, thou God of my salvation: and my tongue shall sing aloud of thy righteousness.

15 O Lord, open thou my lips; and my mouth shall shew forth thy praise.

16 For thou desirest not sacrifice; else would I give it: thou delightest not in burnt offering.

17 The sacrifices of God are a broken spirit: a broken and a contrite heart, O God, thou wilt not despise.

18 Do good in thy good pleasure unto Zion: build thou the walls of Jerusalem.

19 Then shalt thou be pleased with the sacrifices of righteousness, with burnt offering and whole burnt offering: then shall they offer bullocks upon thine altar.

53

1. The fool hath said in his heart, There is no God. Corrupt are they, and have done abominable iniquity: there is none that doeth good.
2. God looked down from heaven upon the children of men, to see if there were any that did understand, that did seek God.
3. Every one of them is gone back: they are altogether become filthy; there is none that doeth good, no, not one.
4. Have the workers of iniquity no knowledge? who eat up my people as they eat bread: they have not called upon God.
5. There were they in great fear, where no fear was: for God hath scattered the bones of him that encampeth against thee: thou hast put them to shame, because God hath despised them.
6. Oh that the salvation of Israel were come out of Zion! When God bringeth back the captivity of his people, Jacob shall rejoice, and Israel shall be glad.

54

1. Save me, O God, by thy name, and judge me by thy strength.
2. Hear my prayer, O God; give ear to the words of my mouth.
3. For strangers are risen up against me, and oppressors seek after my soul: they have not set God before them.
4. Behold, God is mine helper: the Lord is with them that uphold my soul.
5. He shall reward evil unto mine enemies: cut them off in thy truth.
6. I will freely sacrifice unto thee: I will praise thy name, O Lord; for it is good.
7. For he hath delivered me out of all trouble: and mine eye hath seen his desire upon mine enemies.

60

1. O God, thou has cast us off, thou hast scattered us, thou has been displeased; O turn thyself to us again.
2. Thou hast made the earth to tremble; thou hast broken it: heal the breaches thereof; for it shaketh.
3. Thou has shewed thy people hard things: thou hast made us to drink the wine of astonishment.
4. Thou hast given a banner to them that fear thee, that it may be displayed because of the truth.
5. That thy beloved may be delivered; save with thy right hand, and hear me.
6. God hath spoken in his holiness; I will rejoice, I will divide Shechem, and mete out the valley of Succoth.
7. Gilead is mine, and Manasseh is mine; Ephraim also is the strength of mine head; Judah is my lawgiver;
8. Moab is my washpot; over Edom will I cast out my shoe: Philistia, triumph thou because of me.
9. Who will bring me into the strong city? who will lead me into Edom?
10. Wilt not thou, O God, which hadst cast us off? and thou, O God, which didst not go out with our armies?
11. Give us help from trouble: for vain is the help of man.
12. Through God we shall do valiantly: for he it is that shall tread down our enemies.

61

1. Hear my cry, O God; attend unto my prayer.
2. From the end of the earth will I cry unto thee, when my heart is overwhelmed: lead me to the rock that is higher than I.
3. For thou hast been a shelter for me, and a strong tower from the enemy.
4. I will abide in thy tabernacle for ever: I will trust in the covert of thy wings.
5. For thou, O God, hast heard my vows: thou hast given me the heritage of those that fear thy name.
6. Thou wilt prolong the king's life: and his years as many generations.
7. He shall abide before God for ever: O prepare mercy and truth, which may preserve him.
8. So will I sing praise unto thy name for ever, that I may daily perform my vows.

64

1. Hear my voice, O God, in my prayer: preserve my life from fear of the enemy.
2. Hide me from the secret counsel of the wicked; from the insurrection of the workers of iniquity:
3. Who whet their tongue like a sword, and bend their bows to shoot their arrows, even bitter words:
4. That they may shoot in secret at the perfect: suddenly do they shoot at him, and fear not.
5. They encourage themselves in an evil matter: they commune of laying snares privily; they say, Who shall see them?
6. They search out iniquities; they accomplish a diligent search: both the inward thought of every one of them, and the heart, is deep.
7. But God shall shoot at them with an arrow; suddenly shall they be wounded.
8. So they shall make their own tongue to fall upon themselves: all that see them shall flee away.
9. And all men shall fear, and shall declare the work of God; for they shall wisely consider of his doing.
10. The righteous shall be glad in the Lord, and shall trust in him; and all the upright in heart shall glory.

70

1. Make haste, O God, to deliver me; make haste to help me, O Lord.
2. Let them be ashamed and confounded that seek after my soul: let them be turned backward, and put to confusion, that desire my hurt.
3. Let them be turned back for a reward of their shame that say, Aha, aha.
4. Let all those that seek thee rejoice and be glad in thee: and let such as love thy salvation say continually, Let God be magnified.
5. But I am poor and needy: make haste unto me, O God: thou art my help and my deliverer; O Lord, make no tarrying.

77

1 I cried unto God with my voice, even unto God with my voice; and he gave ear unto me.
2 In the day of my trouble I sought the Lord: my sore ran in the night, and ceased not: my soul refused to be comforted.
3 I remembered God, and was troubled: I complained, and my spirit was overwhelmed.
4 Thou holdest mine eyes waking: I am so troubled that I cannot speak.
5 I have considered the days of old, the years of ancient times.
6 I call to remembrance my song in the night; I commune with mine own heart: and my spirit made diligent search.
7 Will the Lord cast off for ever? and will he be favourable no more?
8 Is his mercy clean gone for ever? doth his promise fail for evermore?
9 Hath God forgotten to be gracious? hath he in anger shut up his tender mercies?
10 And I said, This is my infirmity: but I will remember the years of the right hand of the most High.
11 I will remember the works of the Lord: surely I will remember thy wonders of old.

12 I will meditate also of all thy work, and talk of thy doings.
13 Thy way, O God, is in the sanctuary: who is so great a God as our God?
14 Thou art the God that doest wonders: thou hast declared thy strength among the people.
15 Thou hast with thine arm redeemed thy people, the sons of Jacob and Joseph.
16 The waters saw thee, O God, the waters saw thee; they were afraid: the depths also were troubled.
17 The clouds poured out water: the skies sent out a sound: thine arrows also went abroad.
18 The voice of thy thunder was in the heaven: the lightnings lightened the world: the earth trembled and shook.
19 Thy way is in the sea, and thy path in the great waters, and thy footsteps are not known.
20 Thou leddest thy people like a flock by the hand of Moses and Aaron.

79

1 O God, the heathen are come into thine inheritance; thy holy temple have they defiled; they have laid Jerusalem on heaps.
2 The dead bodies of thy servants have they given to be meat unto the fowls of the heaven, the flesh of thy saints unto the beasts of the earth.
3 Their blood have they shed like water round about Jerusalem; and there was none to bury them.
4 We are become a reproach to our neighbours, a scorn and derision to them that are round about us.
5 How long, Lord? wilt thou be angry for ever? shall thy jealousy burn like fire?
6 Pour out thy wrath upon the heathen that have not known thee, and upon the kingdoms that have not called upon thy name.
7 For they have devoured Jacob, and laid waste his dwelling place.
8 O remember not against us former iniquities: let thy tender mercies speedily prevent us: for we are brought very low.
9 Help us, O God of our salvation, for the glory of thy name: and deliver us, and purge away our sins, for thy name's sake.

10 Wherefore should the heathen say, Where is their God? let him be known among the heathen in our sight by the revenging of the blood of thy servants which is shed.
11 Let the sighing of the prisoner come before thee; according to the greatness of thy power preserve thou those that are appointed to die;
12 And render unto our neighbours sevenfold into their bosom their reproach, wherewith they have reproached thee, O Lord.
13 So we thy people and sheep of thy pasture will give thee thanks for ever: we will shew forth thy praise to all generations.

83

1 Keep not thou silence, O God: hold not thy peace, and be not still, O God.
2 For, lo, thine enemies make a tumult: and they that hate thee have lifted up the head.
3 They have taken crafty counsel against thy people, and consulted against thy hidden ones.
4 They have said, Come, and let us cut them off from being a nation; that the name of Israel may be no more in remembrance.
5 For they have consulted together with one consent: they are confederate against thee:
6 The tabernacles of Edom, and the Ishmaelites; of Moab, and the Hagarenes;
7 Gebal, and Ammon, and Amalek; the Philistines with the inhabitants of Tyre;
8 Assur also is joined with them: they have holpen the children of Lot.
9 Do unto them as unto the Midianites; as to Sisera, as to Jabin, at the brook of Kison:
10 Which perished at Endor: they became as dung for the earth.
11 Make their nobles like Oreb, and like Zeeb: yea, all their princes as Zebah, and as Zalmunna:
12 Who said, Let us take to ourselves the houses of God in possession.

13 O my God, make them like a wheel; as the stubble before the wind.
14 As the fire burneth a wood, and as the flame setteth the mountains on fire:
15 So persecute them with thy tempest, and make them afraid with thy storm.
16 Fill their faces with shame; that they may seek thy name, O Lord.
17 Let them be confounded and troubled for ever; yea, let them be put to shame, and perish:
18 That men may know that thou, whose name alone is Jehovah, art the most high over all the earth.

86

1 Bow down thine ear, O Lord, hear me: for I am poor and needy.
2 Preserve my soul; for I am holy; O thou my God, save thy servant that trusteth in thee.
3 Be merciful unto me, O Lord: for I cry unto thee daily.
4 Rejoice the soul of thy servant: for unto thee, O Lord, do I lift up my soul.
5 For thou, Lord, art good, and ready to forgive; and plenteous in mercy unto all them that call upon thee.
6 Give ear, O Lord, unto my prayer; and attend to the voice of my supplications.
7 In the day of my trouble I will call upon thee: for thou wilt answer me.
8 Among the gods there is none like unto thee, O Lord; neither are there any works like unto thy works.
9 All nations whom thou hast made shall come and worship before thee, O Lord; and shall glorify thy name.
10 For thou art great, and doest wondrous things: thou art God alone.
11 Teach me thy way, O Lord; I will walk in thy truth: unite my heart to fear thy name.
12 I will praise thee, O Lord my God, with all my heart; and I will glorify thy name for evermore.
13 For great is thy mercy toward me; and thou hast delivered my soul from the lowest hell.

14 O God, the proud are risen against me, and the assemblies of violent men have sought after my soul; and have not set thee before them.
15 But thou, O Lord, art a God full of compassion, and gracious, longsuffering, and plenteous in mercy and truth.
16 O turn unto me, and have mercy upon me; give thy strength unto thy servant, and save the son of thine handmaid.
17 Shew me a token for good; that they which hate me may see it, and be ashamed: because thou, Lord, hast holpen me, and comforted me.

88

1 O Lord God of my salvation, I have cried day and night before thee:
2 Let my prayer come before thee: incline thine ear unto my cry;
3 For my soul is full of troubles: and my life draweth nigh unto the grave.
4 I am counted with them that go down into the pit: I am as a man that hath no strength:
5 Free among the dead, like the slain that lie in the grave, whom thou rememberest no more: and they are cut off from thy hand.
6 Thou hast laid me in the lowest pit, in darkness, in the deeps.
7 Thy wrath lieth hard upon me, and thou hast afflicted me with all thy waves.
8 Thou hast put away mine acquaintance far from me; thou hast made me an abomination unto them: I am shut up, and I cannot come forth.
9 Mine eye mourneth by reason of affliction: Lord, I have called daily upon thee, I have stretched out my hands unto thee.
10 Wilt thou shew wonders to the dead? shall the dead arise and praise thee?
11 Shall thy loving kindness be declared in the grave? or thy faithfulness in destruction?

12 Shall thy wonders be known in the dark: and thy righteousness in the land of forgetfulness?
13 But unto thee have I cried, O Lord; and in the morning shall my prayer prevent thee.
14 Lord, why castest thou off my soul? why hidest thou thy face from me?
15 I am afflicted and ready to die from my youth up: while I suffer thy terrors I am distracted.
16 Thy fierce wrath goeth over me; thy terrors have cut me off.
17 They came round about me daily like water; they compassed me about together.
18 Lover and friend hast thou put far from me, and mine acquaintance into darkness.

120

1. In my distress I cried unto the Lord, and he heard me.
2. Deliver my soul, O Lord, from lying lips, and from a deceitful tongue.
3. What shall be given unto thee? or what shall be done unto thee, thou false tongue?
4. Sharp arrows of the mighty, with coals of juniper.
5. Woe is me, that I sojourn in Mesech, that I dwell in the tents of Kedar!
6. My soul hath long dwelt with him that hateth peace.
7. I am for peace: but when I speak, they are for war.

123

1 Unto thee lift I up mine eyes, O thou that dwellest in the heavens.
2 Behold, as the eyes of servants look unto the hand of their masters, and as the eyes of a maiden unto the hand of her mistress; so our eyes wait upon the Lord our God, until that he have mercy upon us.
3 Have mercy upon us, O Lord, have mercy upon us: for we are exceedingly filled with contempt.
4 Our soul is exceedingly filled with the scorning of those that are at ease, and with the contempt of the proud.

137

1. By the rivers of Babylon, there we sat down, yea, we wept, when we remembered Zion.
2. We hanged our harps upon the willows in the midst thereof.
3. For there they that carried us away captive required of us a song; and they that wasted us required of us mirth, saying, Sing us one of the songs of Zion.
4. How shall we sing the Lord's song in a strange land?
5. If I forget thee, O Jerusalem, let my right hand forget her cunning.
6. If I do not remember thee, let my tongue cleave to the roof of my mouth; if I prefer not Jerusalem above my chief joy.
7. Remember, O Lord, the children of Edom in the day of Jerusalem; who said, Rase it, rase it, even to the foundation thereof.
8. O daughter of Babylon, who art to be destroyed; happy shall he be, that rewardeth thee as thou hast served us.
9. Happy shall he be, that taketh and dasheth thy little ones against the stones.

142

1. I cried unto the Lord with my voice; with my voice unto the Lord did I make my supplication.
2. I poured out my complaint before him; I shewed before him my trouble.
3. When my spirit was overwhelmed within me, then thou knewest my path. In the way wherein I walked have they privily laid a snare for me.
4. I looked on my right hand, and beheld, but there was no man that would know me: refuge failed me; no man cared for my soul.
5. I cried unto thee, O Lord: I said, Thou art my refuge and my portion in the land of the living.
6. Attend unto my cry; for I am brought very low: deliver me from my persecutors; for they are stronger than I.
7. Bring my soul out of prison, that I may praise thy name: the righteous shall compass me about; for thou shalt deal bountifully with me.

143

1 Hear my prayer, O Lord, give ear to my supplications: in thy faithfulness answer me, and in thy righteousness.
2 And enter not into judgment with thy servant: for in thy sight shall no man living be justified.
3 For the enemy hath persecuted my soul; he hath smitten my life down to the ground; he hath made me to dwell in darkness, as those that have been long dead.
4 Therefore is my spirit overwhelmed within me; my heart within me is desolate.
5 I remember the days of old; I meditate on all thy works; I muse on the work of thy hands.
6 I stretch forth my hands unto thee: my soul thirsteth after thee, as a thirsty land.
7 Hear me speedily, O Lord: my spirit faileth: hide not thy face from me, lest I be like unto them that go down into the pit.
8 Cause me to hear thy loving kindness in the morning; for in thee do I trust: cause me to know the way wherein I should walk; for I lift up my soul unto thee.
9 Deliver me, O Lord, from mine enemies: I flee unto thee to hide me.
10 Teach me to do thy will; for thou art my God: thy spirit is good; lead me into the land of uprightness.
11 Quicken me, O Lord, for thy name's sake: for thy righteousness' sake bring my soul out of trouble.

12 And of thy mercy cut off mine enemies, and destroy all them that afflict my soul: for I am thy servant.

Psalms of Thanksgiving

8

1. O Lord, our Lord, how excellent is thy name in all the earth! who hast set thy glory above the heavens.
2. Out of the mouth of babes and sucklings hast thou ordained strength because of thine enemies, that thou mightest still the enemy and the avenger.
3. When I consider thy heavens, the work of thy fingers, the moon and the stars, which thou hast ordained;
4. What is man, that thou art mindful of him? and the son of man, that thou visitest him?
5. For thou hast made him a little lower than the angels, and hast crowned him with glory and honour.
6. Thou madest him to have dominion over the works of thy hands; thou hast put all things under his feet:
7. All sheep and oxen, yea, and the beasts of the field;
8. The fowl of the air, and the fish of the sea, and whatsoever passeth through the paths of the seas.
9. O Lord, our Lord, how excellent is thy name in all the earth!

16

1. Preserve me, O God: for in thee do I put my trust.
2. O my soul, thou hast said unto the Lord, Thou art my Lord: my goodness extendeth not to thee;
3. But to the saints that are in the earth, and to the excellent, in whom is all my delight.
4. Their sorrows shall be multiplied that hasten after another god: their drink offerings of blood will I not offer, nor take up their names into my lips.
5. The Lord is the portion of mine inheritance and of my cup: thou maintainest my lot.
6. The lines are fallen unto me in pleasant places; yea, I have a goodly heritage.
7. I will bless the Lord, who hath given me counsel: my reins also instruct me in the night seasons.
8. I have set the Lord always before me: because he is at my right hand, I shall not be moved.
9. Therefore my heart is glad, and my glory rejoiceth: my flesh also shall rest in hope.
10. For thou wilt not leave my soul in hell; neither wilt thou suffer thine Holy One to see corruption.
11. Thou wilt shew me the path of life: in thy presence is fulness of joy; at thy right hand there are pleasures for evermore.

23

1. The Lord is my shepherd; I shall not want.
2. He maketh me to lie down in green pastures; he leadeth me beside the still waters.
3. He restoreth my soul: he leadeth me in the paths of righteousness for his name's sake.
4. Yea, though I walk through the valley of the shadow of death, I will fear no evil: for thou art with me; thy rod and thy staff they comfort me.
5. Thou preparest a table before me in the presence of mine enemies: thou anointest my head with oil; my cup runneth over.
6. Surely goodness and mercy shall follow me all the days of my life: and I will dwell in the house of the Lord for ever.

34

1. I will bless the Lord at all times: his praise shall continually be in my mouth.
2. My soul shall make her boast in the Lord: the humble shall hear thereof, and be glad.
3. O magnify the Lord with me, and let us exalt his name together.
4. I sought the Lord, and he heard me, and delivered me from all my fears.
5. They looked unto him, and were lightened: and their faces were not ashamed.
6. This poor man cried, and the Lord heard him, and saved him out of all his troubles.
7. The angel of the Lord encampeth round about them that fear him, and delivereth them.
8. O taste and see that the Lord is good: blessed is the man that trusteth in him.
9. O fear the Lord, ye his saints: for there is no want to them that fear him.
10. The young lions do lack, and suffer hunger: but they that seek the Lord shall not want any good thing.
11. Come, ye children, hearken unto me: I will teach you the fear of the Lord.
12. What man is he that desireth life, and loveth many days, that he may see good?

13 Keep thy tongue from evil, and thy lips from speaking guile.
14 Depart from evil, and do good; seek peace, and pursue it.
15 The eyes of the Lord are upon the righteous, and his ears are open unto their cry.
16 The face of the Lord is against them that do evil, to cut off the remembrance of them from the earth.
17 The righteous cry, and the Lord heareth, and delivereth them out of all their troubles.
18 The Lord is nigh unto them that are of a broken heart; and saveth such as be of a contrite spirit.
19 Many are the afflictions of the righteous: but the Lord delivereth him out of them all.
20 He keepeth all his bones: not one of them is broken.
21 Evil shall slay the wicked: and they that hate the righteous shall be desolate.
22 The Lord redeemeth the soul of his servants: and none of them that trust in him shall be desolate.

63

1 O God, thou art my God; early will I seek thee: my soul thirsteth for thee, my flesh longeth for thee in a dry and thirsty land, where no water is;
2 To see thy power and thy glory, so as I have seen thee in the sanctuary.
3 Because thy loving kindness is better than life, my lips shall praise thee.
4 Thus will I bless thee while I live: I will lift up my hands in thy name.
5 My soul shall be satisfied as with marrow and fatness; and my mouth shall praise thee with joyful lips:
6 When I remember thee upon my bed, and meditate on thee in the night watches.
7 Because thou hast been my help, therefore in the shadow of thy wings will I rejoice.
8 My soul followeth hard after thee: thy right hand upholdeth me.
9 But those that seek my soul, to destroy it, shall go into the lower parts of the earth.
10 They shall fall by the sword: they shall be a portion for foxes.
11 But the king shall rejoice in God; every one that sweareth by him shall glory: but the mouth of them that speak lies shall be stopped.

66

1. Make a joyful noise unto God, all ye lands:
2. Sing forth the honour of his name: make his praise glorious.
3. Say unto God, How terrible art thou in thy works! through the greatness of thy power shall thine enemies submit themselves unto thee.
4. All the earth shall worship thee, and shall sing unto thee; they shall sing to thy name.
5. Come and see the works of God: he is terrible in his doing toward the children of men.
6. He turned the sea into dry land: they went through the flood on foot: there did we rejoice in him.
7. He ruleth by his power for ever; his eyes behold the nations: let not the rebellious exalt themselves.
8. O bless our God, ye people, and make the voice of his praise to be heard:
9. Which holdeth our soul in life, and suffereth not our feet to be moved.
10. For thou, O God, hast proved us: thou hast tried us, as silver is tried.
11. Thou broughtest us into the net; thou laidst affliction upon our loins.
12. Thou hast caused men to ride over our heads; we went through fire and through water: but thou broughtest us out into a wealthy place.

13 I will go into thy house with burnt offerings: I will pay thee my vows.
14 Which my lips have uttered, and my mouth hath spoken, when I was in trouble.
15 I will offer unto thee burnt sacrifices of fatlings, with the incense of rams; I will offer bullocks with goats.
16 Come and hear, all ye that fear God, and I will declare what he hath done for my soul.
17 I cried unto him with my mouth, and he was extolled with my tongue.
18 If I regard iniquity in my heart, the Lord will not hear me:
19 But verily God hath heard me; he hath attended to the voice of my prayer.
20 Blessed be God, which hath not turned away my prayer, nor his mercy from me.

67

1. God be merciful unto us, and bless us; and cause his face to shine upon us.
2. That thy way may be known upon earth, thy saving health among all nations.
3. Let the people praise thee, O God; let all the people praise thee.
4. O let the nations be glad and sing for joy: for thou shalt judge the people righteously, and govern the nations upon earth.
5. Let the people praise thee, O God; let all the people praise thee.
6. Then shall the earth yield her increase; and God, even our own God, shall bless us.
7. God shall bless us; and all the ends of the earth shall fear him.

75

1 Unto thee, O God, do we give thanks, unto thee do we give thanks: for that thy name is near thy wondrous works declare.
2 When I shall receive the congregation I will judge uprightly.
3 The earth and all the inhabitants thereof are dissolved: I bear up the pillars of it.
4 I said unto the fools, Deal not foolishly: and to the wicked, Lift not up the horn:
5 Lift not up your horn on high: speak not with a stiff neck.
6 For promotion cometh neither from the east, nor from the west, nor from the south.
7 But God is the judge: he putteth down one, and setteth up another.
8 For in the hand of the Lord there is a cup, and the wine is red; it is full of mixture; and he poureth out of the same: but the dregs thereof, all the wicked of the earth shall wring them out, and drink them.
9 But I will declare for ever; I will sing praises to the God of Jacob.
10 All the horns of the wicked also will I cut off; but the horns of the righteous shall be exalted.

92

1. It is a good thing to give thanks unto the Lord, and to sing praises unto thy name, O most High:
2. To shew forth thy loving kindness in the morning, and thy faithfulness every night.
3. Upon an instrument of ten strings, and upon the psaltery; upon the harp with a solemn sound.
4. For thou, Lord, has made me glad through thy work: I will triumph in the works of thy hands.
5. O Lord, how great are thy works! and thy thoughts are very deep.
6. A brutish man knoweth not; neither doth a fool understand this.
7. When the wicked spring as the grass, and when all the workers of iniquity do flourish; it is that they shall be destroyed for ever:
8. But thou, Lord, art most high for evermore.
9. For, lo, thine enemies, O Lord, for, lo, thine enemies shall perish; all the workers of iniquity shall be scattered.
10. But my horn shalt thou exalt like the horn of an unicorn: I shall be anointed with fresh oil.
11. Mine eye also shall see my desire on mine enemies, and mine ears shall hear my desire of the wicked that rise up against me.

12 The righteous shall flourish like the palm tree: he shall grow like a cedar in Lebanon.
13 Those that be planted in the house of the Lord shall flourish in the courts of our God.
14 They shall still bring forth fruit in old age; they shall be fat and flourishing;
15 To shew that the Lord is upright: he is my rock, and there is no unrighteousness in him.

95

1. O come, let us sing unto the Lord: let us make a joyful noise to the rock of our salvation.
2. Let us come before his presence with thanksgiving, and make a joyful noise unto him with psalms.
3. For the Lord is a great God, and a great King above all gods.
4. In his hand are the deep places of the earth: the strength of the hills is his also.
5. The sea is his, and he made it: and his hands formed the dry land.
6. O come, let us worship and bow down: let us kneel before the Lord our maker.
7. For he is our God; and we are the people of his pasture, and the sheep of his hand. To day if ye will hear his voice.
8. Harden not your heart, as in the provocation, and as in the day of temptation in the wilderness:
9. When your fathers tempted me, proved me, and saw my work.
10. Forty years long was I grieved with this generation, and said, It is a people that do err in their heart, and they have not known my ways:
11. Unto whom I sware in my wrath that they should not enter into my rest.

100

1. Make a joyful noise unto the Lord, all ye lands.
2. Serve the Lord with gladness: come before his presence with singing.
3. Know ye that the Lord he is God: it is he that hath made us, and not we ourselves; we are his people, and the sheep of his pasture.
4. Enter into his gates with thanksgiving, and into his courts with praise: be thankful unto him, and bless his name.
5. For the Lord is good; his mercy is everlasting; and his truth endureth to all generations.

103

1. Bless the Lord, O my soul: and all that is within me, bless his holy name.
2. Bless the Lord, O my soul, and forget not all his benefits:
3. Who forgiveth all thine iniquities; who healeth all thy diseases;
4. Who redeemeth thy life from destruction; who crowneth thee with loving kindness and tender mercies;
5. Who satisfieth thy mouth with good things; so that thy youth is renewed like the eagle's.
6. The Lord executeth righteousness and judgment for all that are oppressed.
7. He made known his ways unto Moses, his acts unto the children of Israel.
8. The Lord is merciful and gracious, slow to anger, and plenteous in mercy.
9. He will not always chide: neither will he keep his anger for ever.
10. He hath not dealt with us after our sins; nor rewarded us according to our iniquities.
11. For as the heaven is high above the earth, so great is his mercy toward them that fear him.
12. As far as the east is from the west, so far hath he removed our transgressions from us.
13. Like as a father pitieth his children, so the Lord pitieth them that fear him.

14 For he knoweth our frame; he remembereth that we are dust.
15 As for man, his days are as grass: as a flower of the field, so he flourisheth.
16 For the wind passeth over it, and it is gone; and the place thereof shall know it no more.
17 But the mercy of the Lord is from everlasting to everlasting upon them that fear him, and his righteousness unto children's children;
18 To such as keep his covenant, and to those that remember his commandments to do them.
19 The Lord hath prepared his throne in the heavens; and his kingdom ruleth over all.
20 Bless the Lord, ye his angels, that excel in strength, that do his commandments, hearkening unto the voice of his word.
21 Bless ye the Lord, all ye his hosts; ye ministers of his, that do his pleasure.
22 Bless the Lord, all his works in all places of his dominion: bless the Lord, O my soul.

107

1. O give thanks unto the Lord, for he is good: for his mercy endureth for ever.
2. Let the redeemed of the Lord say so, whom he hath redeemed from the hand of the enemy;
3. And gathered them out of the lands, from the east, and from the west, from the north, and from the south.
4. They wandered in the wilderness in a solitary way; they found no city to dwell in.
5. Hungry and thirsty, their soul fainted in them.
6. Then they cried unto the Lord in their trouble, and he delivered them out of their distresses.
7. And he led them forth by the right way, that they might go to a city of habitation.
8. Oh that men would praise the Lord for his goodness, and for his wonderful works to the children of men!
9. For he satisfieth the longing soul, and filleth the hungry soul with goodness.
10. Such as sit in darkness and in the shadow of death, being bound in affliction and iron;
11. Because they rebelled against the words of God, and contemned the counsel of the most High:
12. Therefore he brought down their heart with labour; they fell down, and there was none to help.
13. Then they cried unto the Lord in their trouble, and he saved them out of their distresses.

14 He brought them out of darkness and the shadow of death, and brake their bands in sunder.
15 Oh that men would praise the Lord for his goodness, and for his wonderful works to the children of men!
16 For he hath broken the gates of brass, and cut the bars of iron in sunder.
17 Fools because of their transgression, and because of their iniquities, are afflicted.
18 Their soul abhorreth all manner of meat; and they draw near unto the gates of death.
19 Then they cry unto the Lord in their trouble, and he saveth them out of their distresses.
20 He sent his word, and healed them, and delivered them from their destructions.
21 Oh that men would praise the Lord for his goodness, and for his wonderful works to the children of men!
22 And let them sacrifice the sacrifices of thanksgiving, and declare his works with rejoicing.
23 They that go down to the sea in ships, that do business in great waters;
24 These see the works of the Lord, and his wonders in the deep.
25 For he commandeth, and raiseth the stormy wind, which lifteth up the waves thereof.
26 They mount up to the heaven, they go down again to the depths: their soul is melted because of trouble.
27 They reel to and fro, and stagger like a drunken man, and are at their wit's end.

28 Then they cry unto the Lord in their trouble, and he bringeth them out of their distresses.
29 He maketh the storm a calm, so that the waves thereof are still.
30 Then are they glad because they be quiet; so he bringeth them unto their desired haven.
31 Oh that men would praise the Lord for his goodness, and for his wonderful works to the children of men!
32 Let them exalt him also in the congregation of the people, and praise him in the assembly of the elders.
33 He turneth rivers into a wilderness, and the watersprings into dry ground;
34 A fruitful land into barrenness, for the wickedness of them that dwell therein.
35 He turneth the wilderness into a standing water, and dry ground into watersprings.
36 And there he maketh the hungry to dwell, that they may prepare a city for habitation;
37 And sow the fields, and plant vineyards, which may yield fruits of increase.
38 He blesseth them also, so that they are multiplied greatly; and suffereth not their cattle to decrease.
39 Again, they are minished and brought low through oppression, affliction, and sorrow.
40 He poureth contempt upon princes, and causeth them to wander in the wilderness, where there is no way.
41 Yet setteth he the poor on high from affliction, and maketh him families like a flock.

42 The righteous shall see it, and rejoice: and all iniquity shall stop her mouth.
43 Whoso is wise, and will observe these things, even they shall understand the loving kindness of the Lord.

111

1. Praise ye the Lord. I will praise the Lord with my whole heart, in the assembly of the upright, and in the congregation.
2. The works of the Lord are great, sought out of all them that have pleasure therein.
3. His work is honourable and glorious: and his righteousness endureth for ever.
4. He hath made his wonderful works to be remembered: the Lord is gracious and full of compassion.
5. He hath given meat unto them that fear him: he will ever be mindful of his covenant.
6. He hath shewed his people the power of his works, that he may give them the heritage of the heathen.
7. The works of his hands are verity and judgment; all his commandments are sure.
8. They stand fast for ever and ever, and are done in truth and uprightness.
9. He sent redemption unto his people: he hath commanded his covenant for ever: holy and reverend is his name.
10. The fear of the Lord is the beginning of wisdom: a good understanding have all they that do his commandments: his praise endureth for ever.

113

1 Praise ye the Lord, Praise, O ye servants of the Lord, praise the name of the Lord.
2 Blessed be the name of the Lord from this time forth and for evermore.
3 From the rising of the sun unto the going down of the same the Lord's name is to be praised.
4 The Lord is high above all nations, and his glory above the heavens.
5 Who is like unto the Lord our God, who dwelleth on high.
6 Who humbleth himself to behold the things that are in heaven, and in the earth!
7 He raiseth up the poor out of the dust, and lifteth the needy out of the dunghill;
8 That he may set him with princes, even with the princes of his people.
9 He maketh the barren woman to keep house, and to be a joyful mother of children. Praise ye the Lord.

116

1. I love the Lord, because he hath heard my voice and my supplications.
2. Because he hath inclined his ear unto me, therefore will I call upon him as long as I live.
3. The sorrows of death compassed me, and the pains of hell gat hold upon me: I found trouble and sorrow.
4. Then called I upon the name of the Lord; O Lord, I beseech thee, deliver my soul.
5. Gracious is the Lord, and righteous; yea, our God is merciful.
6. The Lord preserveth the simple: was brought low, and he helped me.
7. Return unto thy rest, O my soul; for the Lord hath dealt bountifully with thee.
8. For thou hast delivered my soul from death, mine eyes from tears, and my feet from falling.
9. I will walk before the Lord in the land of the living.
10. I believed, therefore have I spoken: I was greatly afflicted:
11. I said in my haste, All men are liars.
12. What shall I render unto the Lord for all his benefits toward me?
13. I will take the cup of salvation, and call upon the name of the Lord.
14. I will pay my vows unto the Lord now in the presence of all his people.

15 Precious in the sight of the Lord is the death of his saints.
16 O Lord, truly I am thy servant; I am thy servant, and the son of thine handmaid: thou hast loosed my bonds.
17 I will offer to thee the sacrifice of thanksgiving, and will call upon the name of the Lord.
18 I will pay my vows unto the Lord now in the presence of all his people.
19 In the courts of the Lord's house, in the midst of thee, O Jerusalem. Praise ye the Lord.

124

1. If it had not been the Lord who was on our side, now may Israel say;
2. If it had not been the Lord who was on our side, when men rose up against us:
3. Then they had swallowed us up quick, when their wrath was kindled against us:
4. Then the waters had overwhelmed us, the stream had gone over our soul:
5. Then the proud waters had gone over our soul.
6. Blessed be the Lord, who hath not given us as a prey to their teeth.
7. Our soul is escaped as a bird out of the snare of the fowlers: the snare is broken, and we are escaped.
8. Our help is in the name of the Lord, who made heaven and earth.

138

1 I will praise thee with my whole heart: before the gods will I sing praise unto thee.
2 I will worship toward thy holy temple, and praise thy name for thy loving kindness and for thy truth: for thou hast magnified thy word above all thy name.
3 In the day when I cried thou answeredst me, and strengthenedst me with strength in my soul.
4 All the kings of the earth shall praise thee, O Lord, when they hear the words of thy mouth.
5 Yea, they shall sing in the ways of the Lord: for great is the glory of the Lord.
6 Though the Lord be high, yet hath he respect unto the lowly: but the proud he knoweth afar off.
7 Though I walk in the midst of trouble, thou wilt revive me: thou shalt stretch forth thine hand against the wrath of mine enemies, and thy right hand shall save me.
8 The Lord will perfect that which concerneth me: thy mercy, O Lord, endureth for ever: forsake not the works of thine own hands.

146

1. Praise ye the Lord. Praise the Lord, O my soul.
2. While I live will I praise the Lord: I will sing praises unto my God while I have any being.
3. Put not your trust in princes, nor in the son of man, in whom there is no help.
4. His breath goeth forth, he returneth to his earth; in that very day his thoughts perish.
5. Happy is he that hath the God of Jacob for his help, whose hope is in the Lord his God:
6. Which made heaven, and earth, the sea, and all that therein is: which keepeth truth for ever:
7. Which executeth judgment for the oppressed: which giveth food to the hungry. The Lord looseth the prisoners:
8. The Lord openeth the eyes of the blind: the Lord raiseth them that are bowed down: the Lord loveth the righteous:
9. The Lord preserveth the strangers; he relieveth the fatherless and widow: but the way of the wicked he turneth upside down.
10. The Lord shall reign for ever, even thy God, O Zion, unto all generations. Praise ye the Lord.

150

1. Praise ye the Lord. Praise God in his sanctuary: praise him in the firmament of his power.
2. Praise him for his mighty acts: praise him according to his excellent greatness.
3. Praise him with the sound of the trumpet: praise him with the psaltery and harp.
4. Praise him with the timbrel and dance: praise him with stringed instruments and organs.
5. Praise him upon the loud cymbals: praise him upon the high sounding cymbals.
6. Let every thing that hath breath praise the Lord. Praise ye the Lord.

Index of First Lines

Behold, bless ye the Lord, all ye servants of the Lord, which by night stand in the house of the Lord.	38
Behold, how good and how pleasant it is for brethren to dwell together in unity!	37
Bless the Lord, O my soul: and all that is within me, bless his holy name.	105
Blessed is every one that feareth the Lord; that walketh in his ways.	36
Blessed is the man that walketh not in the counsel of the ungodly, nor standeth in the way of sinners, nor sitteth in the seat of the scornful.	5
Bow down thine ear, O Lord, hear me: for I am poor and needy.	78
By the rivers of Babylon, there we sat down, yea, we wept, when we remembered Zion.	84
Except the Lord build the house, they labour in vain that build it: except the Lord keep the city, the watchman waketh but in vain.	35
Give unto the Lord, O ye mighty, give unto the Lord glory and strength.	8
God be merciful unto us, and bless us; and cause his face to shine upon us.	99

God is our refuge and strength, a very present help in trouble.	11
God standeth in the congregation of the mighty; he judgeth among the gods.	24
Great is the Lord, and greatly to be praised in the city of our God, in the mountain of his holiness.	13
Have mercy upon me, O God, according to thy loving kindness: according unto the multitude of thy tender mercies blot out my transgressions.	64
Hear me when I call, O God of my righteousness: thou hast enlarged me when I was in distress; have mercy upon me, and hear my prayer.	42
Hear my cry, O God; attend unto my prayer.	69
Hear my prayer, O Lord, give ear to my supplications: in thy faithfulness answer me, and in thy righteousness.	86
Hear my voice, O God, in my prayer: preserve my life from fear of the enemy.	70
Hear the right, O Lord, attend unto my cry, give ear unto my prayer, that goeth not out of feigned lips.	51
Hear this, all ye people; give ear, all ye inhabitants of the world:	15
How amiable are thy tabernacles, O Lord of hosts!	25
How long wilt thou forget me, O Lord? for ever? how long wilt thou hide thy face from me?	50

I cried unto God with my voice, even unto God with my voice; and he gave ear unto me.	72
I cried unto the Lord with my voice; with my voice unto the Lord did I make my supplication.	85
I love the Lord, because he hath heard my voice and my supplications.	113
I was glad when they said unto me, Let us go into the house of the Lord.	34
I will bless the Lord at all times: his praise shall continually be in my mouth.	94
I will praise thee with my whole heart: before the gods will I sing praise unto thee.	116
I will praise thee, O Lord, with my whole heart; I will shew forth all thy marvellous works.	46
I will sing of mercy and judgment: unto thee, O Lord, will I sing.	32
If it had not been the Lord who was on our side, now may Israel say;	115
In my distress I cried unto the Lord, and he heard me.	82
In thee, O Lord, do I put my trust; let me never be ashamed: deliver me in thy righteousness.	61
It is a good thing to give thanks unto the Lord, and to sing praises unto thy name, O most High:	101
Judge me, O Lord; for I have walked in mine integrity: I have trusted also in the Lord; therefore I shall not slide.	58

Keep not thou silence, O God: hold not thy peace, and be not still, O God.	76
Lord, how are they increased that rouble me! many are they that rise up against me.	41
Make a joyful noise unto God, all ye lands:	97
Make a joyful noise unto the Lord, all ye lands.	104
Make haste, O God, to deliver me; make haste to help me, O Lord.	71
My God, my God, why hast thou forsaken me? why art thou so far from helping me, and from the words of my roaring?	53
My heart is inditing a good matter: I speak of the things which I have made touching the king: my tongue is the pen of a ready writer.	9
O clap your hands, all ye people; shout unto God with the voice of triumph.	12
O come, let us sing unto the Lord: let us make a joyful noise to the rock of our salvation.	103
O give thanks unto the Lord, for he is good; for his mercy endureth for ever.	107
O God, the heathen are come into thine inheritance; thy holy temple have they defiled; they have laid Jerusalem on heaps.	74
O God, thou art my God; early will I seek thee: my soul thirsteth for thee, my flesh longeth for thee in a dry and thirsty land, where no water is;	96

O God, thou has cast us off, thou hast scattered us, thou has been displeased; O turn thyself to us again.	68
O Lord God of my salvation, I have cried day and night before thee:	80
O lord my God, in thee do I put my trust: save me from all them that persecute me, and deliver me:	44
O Lord, our Lord, how excellent is thy name in all the earth! who hast set thy glory above the heavens.	91
O lord rebuke me not in thine anger, neither chasten me in thy hot displeasure.	43
O sing unto the Lord a new song: sing unto the Lord, all the earth.	28
O sing unto the Lord a new song; for he hath done marvellous things: his right hand, and his holy arm, hath gotten him the victory.	31
Praise ye the Lord, Praise, O ye servants of the Lord, praise the name of the Lord.	112
Praise ye the Lord. Blessed is the man that feareth the Lord, that delighteth greatly in his commandments.	33
Praise ye the Lord. I will praise the Lord with my whole heart, in the assembly of the upright, and in the congregation.	111
Praise ye the Lord. Praise God in his sanctuary: praise him in the firmament of his power.	118
Praise ye the Lord. Praise the Lord, O my soul.	117

Preserve me, O God: for in thee do I put my trust.	92
Save me, O God, by thy name, and judge me by thy strength.	67
Sing aloud unto God our strength: make a joyful noise unto the God of Jacob.	22
The earth is the Lord's, and the fulness thereof; the world, and they that dwell therein.	7
The fool hath said in his heart, There is no God. Corrupt are they, and have done abominable iniquity: there is none that doeth good.	66
The Lord is my light and my salvation; whom shall I fear? the Lord is the strength of my life; of whom shall I be afraid?	59
The Lord is my shepherd; I shall not want.	93
The Lord reigneth, he is clothed with majesty; the Lord is clothed with strength, wherewith he hath girded himself: the world also is established, that it cannot be moved.	27
The Lord reigneth; let the earth rejoice; let the multitude of isles be glad thereof.	30
The mighty God, even the Lord, hath spoken, and called the earth from the rising of the sun unto the going down thereof.	17
Truly God is good to Israel, even to such as are of a clean heart.	19

Unto thee lift I up mine eyes, O thou that dwellest in the heavens.	83
Unto thee, O God, do we give thanks, unto thee do we give thanks: for that thy name is near thy wondrous works declare.	100
Unto thee, O Lord, do I lift up my soul.	56
Why do the heathen rage, and the people imagine a vain thing?	6
Why standest thou afar off, O lord? why hidest thou thyself in times of trouble?	48